The Magic of Patience

The Magic of Patience

A Jataka Tale

Illustrated by Rosalyn White

DHARMA PUBLISHING

First published 1989

Second edition 2009, augmented with guidance
for parents and teachers

Printed on acid-free paper

Printed in the United States of America by Dharma Press
35788 Hauser Bridge Road, Cazadero, California 95421

1   2   3   4   5   6   7   8   9

Library of Congress Cataloging-in-Publication Data

Magic of Patience

(Jataka Tales Series)
Summary: Buffalo persists in being kind and patient with a mischievous
monkey, despite his annoying tricks.

Jataka stories, English. [1. Jataka stories]
I. White, Rosalyn, ill. II. Series
BQ1462.E5 M34 1989   294.3'823   83-33442

ISBN 978-0-89800-427-4

Dedicated to children everywhere

Once upon a time deep within a jungle in the far-off land of India, there lived a Great Being in the form of a wild buffalo. On the outside the buffalo was stern and intimidating, but on the inside he had a gentle and wise heart. In the same jungle lived a mischievous monkey whose life's goal was to tease the buffalo, which he did day and night.

Whenever the buffalo was about to feed on some tasty green grass, the monkey liked to play a trick on him. "Try and eat! Try and eat! Even though I am sitting right under your feet!"

When the buffalo went to the river to take a refreshing bath, the monkey played a different prank on him; "Don't slip and fall! Don't slip and fall! Even though you cannot see at all!"

When the buffalo was getting ready to take a well-deserved nap, the mischievous monkey would jump up and down on his back, to keep him from dozing off. "Give me a ride! Give me a ride! Or my stick will beat your hide!"

Still the buffalo was never harsh with the monkey, and never even tried to frighten him away. He patiently endured the monkey's antics and always treated him kindly.

One day a magical forest sprite caught sight of the monkey playing his antics and became angry. "O great buffalo, why do you put up with this silly game? What are you thinking? Are you afraid of this monkey? Have you become his slave? Does he perhaps know some terrible secret about you that he threatens to tell? The strongest lions fear your wrath! Even elephants step out of your path! With these hooves of yours, you could crush him to bits! With these horns of yours, you could shred him to strips!"

"O forest sprite," the buffalo replied, "anger never leads to happiness. In fact, the monkey is doing me a great favor by giving me an opportunity to overcome my anger and practice patience. By learning to be kind, I am protecting myself as well as others. How peaceful I feel inside when I am patient. Anger would only upset my heart; I might even hurt someone and feel sorry later."

The forest sprite still did not understand. "Really! This rascal's tricks will only worsen if you don't wise up fast and teach him a lesson!"

"Believe me, my friend, it is better to be patient. Who knows if patience may awaken his inner feelings? You may be right, he is a silly monkey. But just like all creatures, he possesses a true heart."

The forest sprite was amazed. Even though he was familiar with all manner of magic and spells, he had not yet figured out how to handle a tease. "Patience! What is that? It must be a magical charm! Could you teach me how to do it? Show me quickly! Show me now!"

"To practice patience," replied the buffalo, "you need help from a real rascal. It's no use practicing on gentle and kind creatures who require no patience at all. No, what you need is a real monkey. Would you like to use mine?"

"Monkey! That tease? If he tried his silly tricks on me, I'd show him some of mine!"

"Well, you see how hard it is to have patience. But please keep trying, for it is indeed like a magical charm."

The buffalo continued, "I learned to be patient by thinking about the monkey. One day his teasing will surely get him in trouble. Sooner or later he will anger some quick-tempered creature who will give him a bad scare or a serious beating. Poor monkey! And I imagined how lonely he must be. None of the animals want him around, and everyone pushes him away. Poor monkey! Then I thought about how confused he is. He relies on bad qualities instead of good ones, turning all his cleverness and energy into foolish tricks. I feel sorry for the monkey and do not wish to cause him even more misery."

"Imagine!" said the forest sprite. "If I learn to think it through the way you do, then maybe I will learn patience too."

And off flew the forest sprite, eager to practice this wonderful charm called patience.

Just then the monkey, who had been hiding in the trees listening to every word, came up to the buffalo and said, "O dear buffalo, I did not know I had such a good friend. In fact, I did not think I had any friends at all. How kind and strong you are to be patient with a naughty monkey like me. Please forgive me for teasing you and playing mean tricks, and let me be your friend."

If you think of all beings as your friends,
tricks and teasing can do you no harm,
for your heart is protected by patience
and patience works like a charm!

My page

Colored by _____

The Jataka stories are intended to nurture in readers young and old an appreciation for values shared by all the world's great spiritual traditions; values such as kindness, forgiveness, compassion, humility, courage, honesty and patience. This story can be a bridge to the children in your life and help open a dialogue that you can both enjoy.

The Magic of Patience

A gentle buffalo is teased daily by a mischievous monkey. Of course the buffalo could easily drive the monkey away, but he chooses not to. While the other animals in the forest shun the monkey, the buffalo remains kind and patient. Finally, the monkey learns that the buffalo's patience comes not from weakness, but rather from the strength of his love. The buffalo's gentle attitude inspires the monkey to change his ways and to be caring and kind to all other animals.

Key Values
Kindness
Patience
Sensitivity

Questions to promote learning

Engage the children by asking at the turning of a page: "What do you think will happen next?"

Asking questions about the events and values in the story will deepen their understanding and enrich their vocabulary. For example:

- Why do the jungle animals avoid the monkey?
- What tricks does the monkey play?
- Can you remember a situation when you found it hard to be patient?
- Why does the forest sprite want to learn patience?
- What helps you to be patient?
- Is there someone who teases you and often tries to get your attention?
- What is a good way to handle a tease?

Discussion topics and questions can be modified depending on the age of your child.

Learning through play

Children enjoy trying out new ideas, using all five senses to make discoveries. After providing the materials, the time and space for play, encourage their creativity and watch them explore. Play with the characters:

- Have the children color in or draw a scene or character that intrigues them. Then invite them to talk about what it means to them, exploring the key values.
- Make masks for each character in the story.
- Paint the masks and decorate them.
- Have each child choose a character to impersonate. Imitating the voices, bring the qualities and postures of the monkey, the buffalo and the forest sprite to life. Then switch roles.
- Display the key values somewhere visible and refer to them in the course of the day,
- Make up your own story about a tease; ask the child how it would handle the situation.

Reading tips

- Even before children can read, they enjoy storybooks and love growing familiar with the characters and drawings. You can show them the pictures in this book and tell the story in your own words.
- Some Jatakas include difficult concepts. You can prepare by going over the book alone first. By reading the book to the children more than once and helping them to recognize words, you help them to build vocabulary.
- Children love to hear the same story with different and sometimes exaggerated voices for each character.
- Carry a book whenever you leave the house in case there is some extra time for reading.
- Talk about the story with the children while you are all engaged in daily activities like washing the dishes or driving to school.
- Display the key values somewhere visible and refer to them in your daily interactions.

Names and places

India: The source of many spiritual traditions and the background of most of the Jatakas (accounts of the Buddha's previous lives). People seeking wisdom have always viewed India's forests and jungles as favorable places for solitary retreats. The Buddha taught the Jatakas to clarify the workings of karma, the relationship between actions and results.

The forest sprite: According to most spiritual traditions, nature spirits exist in a world parallel to our own, and their task is to protect the environment. They can be quite powerful. In myths they are portrayed as personal beings.

The Jataka tales are folk tales that were transmitted orally, memorized and passed from generation to generation for hundreds of years. We are grateful for the opportunity to offer them to you. May they inspire fresh insight into the dynamics of human relationships and may understanding grow with each reading.

JATAKA TALES SERIES